It is abou

Mindfulness in a busy world

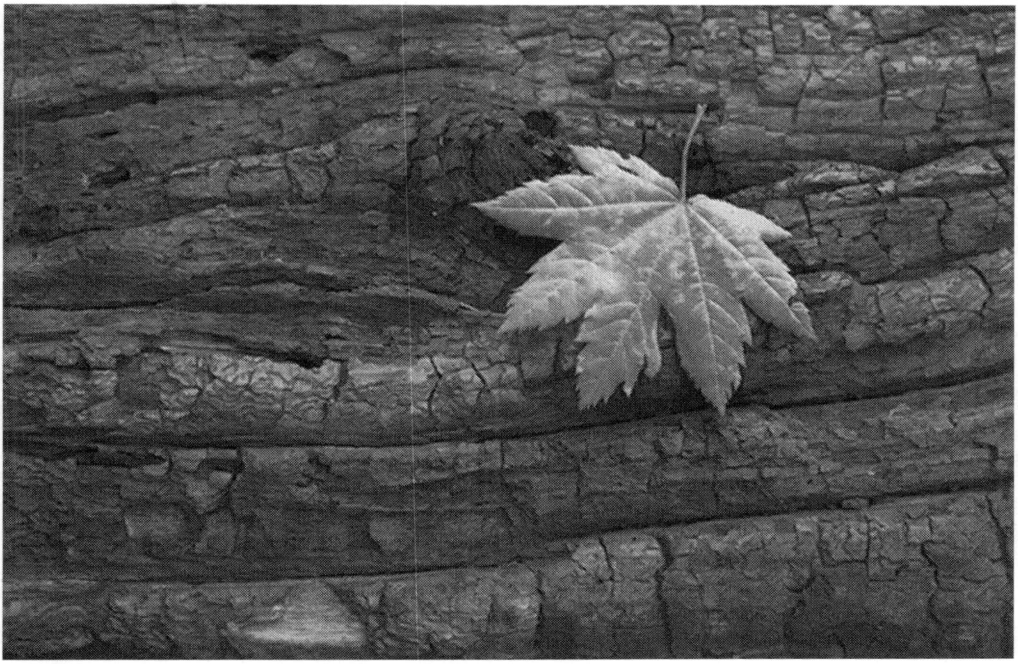

Author: Harwinder S.
Editor & Illustrator: Pargeet S.

TABLE OF CONTENTS

IT IS ABOUT YOU

Minimizing stress..4
Developing Hobbies...6
Mindfulness..8
Breathing...10
Silence Meditation..12
Awareness...14
Sensory Input..16
A minute a day..17
It is about you TWO..18

It was NEVER about you....................................23
Epilogue 25

IT IS ABOUT YOU

Through this book, I want to communicate what has worked best in our lives by practicing mindfulness as best as we can. We have included our own illustrations for this book.

"If you are lonely when you are alone, you are in bad company" Jean-Paul Sartre

Minimizing Stress

Nowadays everyone is about reducing stress. You label anything as "stress reducing" and people are sure to buy it. This is what I am trying to do here (pun intended). Even though you have read and probably know a lot more about stress busting than I can tell you, you still are sitting on the internet, browsing for more knowledge. In that case, this just might be what you are looking for.

I have read several books on mindfulness and Buddhism trying to find a ritual or schedule that works best or even a simple technique that might be helpful in difficult or stressful situations. I have lived in New York city during most of my adult life so far. I was looking for a shortcut to stress relief. What I found is that, there is none.

You have to adapt daily rituals in your life where you pay full attention to whatever it is that you are doing in that moment. Be it something as simple as your morning coffee or evening walk or sitting with your pets. Take your time and do it care and presence. It has to be done at a set or certain time and with proper care and attention. This simple act that most of us already perform but without much care, can majorly transform our lives.

There are several self-help books written on stress management. But you do not want to manage it, you would ideally want to just reduce or eliminate it, if this was possible.

Just by focusing on managing something negative, you are giving it more weight and in return harming yourself. Focus on the positives in your life. See that bright side.

I have seen many people write or share their favorite quote. The saying or something that speaks to them and. Gives them strength. It can be anything. One of my favorites is by Robert Schuller "tough times never last but tough people do". This is something that people perhaps provides some sort of strength.

I see doors and windows marked with "this too shall pass". It is more of an attitude or a belief that things are going to be back to normal. Especially during the present times when everything seems bleak due to the global pandemic. It is important to know that this too shall pass.

Take Away: Don't sweat it.

Developing hobbies

Science has backed the fact that having a hobby can make you healthier and better at your job. A hobby does not have to be physically demanding. It can be as simple as penning your thoughts down at the end of the day. Or gardening, just maintaining a few pots or pans might be very helpful.

Seeing results with whatever your hobby is will give you more confidence in yourself. It also helps take your mind off for a few minutes a day.

Gardening traditionally works best for people. Reading, bird watching, fishing…pick whichever works. I picked gardening. Each time I buy or grow a plant, I try to study all I can about it. Recently I am trying to venture into bonsai making.

Traditionally only Zen masters used to create these…what better hobby to pick than this. Again writing, reading anything will do. See what works best for you. Calligraphy is another hobby that might seem interesting to the readers and is definitely worth exploring. All you need is black ink and paper.

Many people underestimate the importance of pursuing a hobby. Per their beliefs, it is a waste of their time. The time they can use to work or study or do household chores. Little do they know that with a hobby they will not only still. Be able to do all that needs to be done but with a more relaxed mindset.

According to an article published in the most prestigious scientific journal, Nature[1], hobbies can considerably enhance a researcher's productivity as well as creativity.

What better way to bust stress than do something you love? Many regular chores can be pursued as a hobby too. For. Example cooking or baking. Instead of doing it monotonously as a chore, you can make it a hobby. Cook up some new recipes that you have never tried before or reinvent the already existing one with minor touch ups.

Try to be creative with the exercise you do. Any particular chore that you dread, try to see it in a creative way. See if it is possible to make it fun.

Take Away: Pick a hobby and stick to it.

Mindfulness

According to various sources, paying attention to whatever you are doing in the present moment is known as mindfulness. It seems pretty simple to read and understand. But even while writing this my mind is wandering off in ten different directions. A Buddhist will say that me noticing this is progress. This is just the tip of the iceberg.

We need to constantly bring our attention and focus back to the breath. I have seen most people recommending waking up early to meditate or listen to a mindfulness podcast. However, there are also those who find it more beneficial to practice mindfulness after a stressful day or before bedtime.

I believe few minutes a day during anytime that works for you, will do, as long as it is consistent. I prefer to combine it with my daily ritual already in place. Like morning drive to work or evening tea. Figure out a time that works best for you and take a few minutes to meditate. This will make you better at your job and ensures well-being.

Travel if this is your thing. It is the. Best way to get to know this beautiful planet we are put on.

The renowned Dalai Lama recommends traveling to a new place at least once a year if it is possible. It opens up your mind and takes you physically and mentally away from the chaos. You get to have a moment to relax and rejuvenate. You bring the relaxed you to your family and friends. I believe this is a great piece of advice. If you are unable to do this, then try a creative thing at home, something you have never tried before.

Some people re-organize their rooms or homes. There are many of us who find cleaning calming. In Zen Buddhism, cleaning is given much importance. Zen monks broom the floor as part of their chores and as a way of clearing their head. Do whatever it is that you do with attention and creativity.

It will be rewarding no matter how small it seems. In some military establishments, the cadets are taught to properly make their beds first thing they wake up. This means they have started. The day with one task done right. No reason why all of us should not be doing this. This one task done right first thing in the morning gives you confidence and starts your day on the right note. So make your bed!

Take Away: Take few minutes out of your day to be present.

Breathing

"Feelings come and go like clouds in a windy sky, conscious breathing is my anchor".

Thich Nhat Hanh

Breathing is at the core of the meditation or mindfulness practice. Buddhist belief is that everything is centered around breath.... which could not be more accurate.

Hence, focusing on your breath is one of the core teachings of mindfulness meditation. Some even ask you to follow the breath down to your limbs to "feel" each sensation and sort of check in with your body.

Focus on the breath is crucial is what I am trying to say. Especially during times of difficult emotions. For example, anger. The most feared of them all. When we are angry, we are out of ourselves Hence regret saying or doing anything while mesmerized by anger. It is extremely difficult to just start breathing while you are angry. Therefore, a consistent routine is essential.

You can easily calm your anger if you have been practicing some sort of calming ritual or technique such as mindfulness in your life. Train yourself to focus on your breath. Breathing is the foundation of the Indian practice of Yoga. There are several yoga poses centered on breathing such as Pranayama or kapalbhati (alternate nostril breathing).

The best way to breath is by taking slow and deep breaths. In though the nose and out though the mouth. Start your day or do whenever you see your body is getting tense. Breathe till the tension in the muscles dissipates. As an added bonus drink water. However, drink 40-45 minutes before or after your yoga or meditation.

Recently I came across the importance of "diaphragm" in breathing and building confidence. While researching further, I found out many of us breathe shallow. Our breaths are short and fast. This is not the right way to breathe.

Our breaths need to be deep and engage our diaphragms. If you do not know what a diaphragm is. It is the cartilage layer right below your lungs. A good measure of a deep breathe is to see whether or not your diaphragm is rising and falling as you breathe.

Here is a breathing exercise to practice breathing using diaphragm:

Put your dominant hand on your diaphragm. Just under the lungs.

Take a deep in breath focusing on the hand position.

Feel your hand rising with the inbreath. This is indicative of your diaphragm rising.

Now exhale.

Repeat this process at least 5-10 times to begin with. Then increase time as you feel comfortable.

This breathing exercise will not only improve your anxiety levels but will also help improve your confidence.

Take Away: go back to your diaphragm in difficult times.

Silence Meditation

"speech is silver, silence is golden".

Proverb

Practice not talking or being silent few minutes a day but being fully observant of your surroundings. You hear much more when you do not speak.

Silence strengthens the core. It has been known to. Be very beneficial for overall. Physical and emotional well-being. Some even say it lowers blood pressure. Not sure how true this is. Personally, I do believe that it makes you come out stronger and with well-thought vocabulary. I find it best to be silent during my evening coffee or teatime even if this is just for a few minutes. During this time, I try to pay full attention to my beverage. It is extremely calming.

Being silent in nature is also very rewarding. While on a nature walk, try to pay attention to any bird sounds you hear or any new plants or trees you see. Notice how many sounds can you hear around you. You would be surprised to hear how much noise surrounds us at every given moment.

Sitting next to a waterfall is very soothing. Flowing water sounds have a calming effect on our nerves bringing us back to the moment.

I like to have my morning tea in silence. This gives me time to gather my thoughts. Best practice would be to start with a 10-15 breath breathing exercise. I picked "kapalbhati" (a sharp breathing yoga technique that is done on an empty stomach) or diaphragm. Breathing (described above in the breathing section).

Here is how Kapalbhati (kapala: skull, bhati: shining) is done: Also called as breathe of fire, this exercise helps sharpen your brain.

Site cross legged on the floor or any leveled surface in the meditative posture.

Close your eyes and relax your body.

Inhale deeply through both nostrils and expand your chest area.

Expel the breath with forceful. Contractions of the abdominal muscles. Don't push too forcefully. This should not. Hurt.

Relax. Do not strain.

Continue forceful exhalation with passive inhalation.

Repeat 5-10 times as a beginner and you can increase breaths gradually once you are comfortable.

Take Away: be the silent observer sometimes.

Awareness

Being aware, I think, is another most stressed upon point in mindfulness meditation. In a way, it is the goal you are trying to achieve. The grand prize here is full awareness and presence.

You will make better decisions personally and professionally just by being aware. Silence will be extremely helpful here. The old adage "think before you speak" comes to mind.

Take your time in doing whatever it is that you are tasked with. There is never too much of a rush to not breath. When you are practicing your hobby or your daily ritual, try to pay attention to details.

You might find this helpful for your walks: notice things around you instead of mindlessly rushing to the destination. I read somewhere cats are considered Zen masters (or maybe it was meant as a joke). Cats are very intriguing to people. Like many people, I find them to be very Zen. Whenever I come across a cat and look into its eyes, it seems to be hiding some important knowledge that I do not know (pun intended). Plus, they are funny.

Another important aspect of awareness is to take a step away from technology. There should be no technology time where we ideally switch off or at least put away our electronic devices. Now you can choose to do whatever you want with this time…. just not using electronics.

Read a book, have an essential oil bath, organize your stuff or make some coffee and write your thoughts. It has to be something you love.

Be aware of your thoughts and emotions as you make decisions. The decision could be as simple as deciding what and when to eat? Notice the emotion behind it. Make sure it is hunger and not worry, stress or anger. It is not surprising how many emotions lead us to the refrigerator door.

There is a small exercise you can do. Put a reminder on your fridge to remind yourself early on. Once you gain more awareness you can discard the note. Apply this technique to any area of your life that you feel is overwhelmed by your emotions.

Take Away:

be aware of your surroundings.

Sensory Input

Oftentimes we are mindless about what goes in our minds and surroundings. Concerningly we are unaware of what we are feeding our brain. Too many unhealthy calories, if I may. From the social media to the kind of entertainment we chose to watch. I am not trying to censor anything but when I look around myself…. I see people engrossed in the latest trending videos.

Now this may not necessarily be bad, since this trend is becoming a new way for common people to express themselves and to "report" events, if you must. The concern however is becoming addicted to this type of content. You saw…you learnt…. you should leave it at that. Unless you are some kind of authority to be of help.

But most of us are hooked to this kind of entertainment. I would call it "eGossip". Try to reduce the amount of eGossip you feed. Yourself. Pick your entertainment content wisely. Unless you are Einstein, the rest of us have limited mental energy to work with. I would stress myself less over things beyond my control.

Take Away:

Be mindful of what you are feeding your brain through your eyes.

A minute A day

Now you are probably thinking why buy a book and practice anything. I would argue we are better than the mindfulness apps out there. Mindfulness apps are aiming to become the mcdonalds of meditation industry. They claim that what monks, with decades of experience in the mountains, learnt after abandoning literally "Everything" …. that they can teach you "all that" in 10 minutes or less a day by charging very little money. My advice: Go figure.

Mindfulness apps have worked for me personally but only for a MONTH. Then again you and I are different. My problem with the app was that I needed technology to be present in my own body and my own life. Slightly crippling, I thought, as I noticed one day that how desperately I wanted to do my 10-minute meditation and just avoid the rest of the events of the day.

I subconsciously started to "cling" to the app. I could only meditate for 10 minutes and only with the App. I would. Not completely trash them either. For someone who is a "beginner" these apps do a great job to get you initiated or started on the path to mindfulness. But you need to be able to step away from the app and be able to do the 10-minutes mindfulness by yourself after a certain period of time. I would assume that would and should be the ultimate goal of these apps anyway!

Take Away:

Don't let the means be the mains.

It is about you TWO: Mindfulness in relationships

Mindfulness is extremely beneficial when. It comes to relationships. Any and all types of bonds are strengthened by a little dose of attention in your behaviors and actions. Small acts of appreciation in relationships will turn out to be big future investments.

When things are tense, a small sorry or asking, "how can I help?" can go a long way.

Other things that can be useful are sharing activity/activities together. For example, go for nature walks together. Or go the gym together. Have a common coffee or teatime. Be there in the moment.

If one of you has a. passion or hobby, try to be enthusiastic and participate by showing interest if you can. Also, it is crucial to have your own hobby as well. Nothing compulsory and it can be as simple as going for walks so your hobby could be walking or having coffee or tea at a certain time in a certain way etc. while being mindful. Simply pick something that you already do and make it better.

Take Away:

Engage each other in productivity.

Zen illustration by Pargeet S.

Zen illustration by Pargeet S.

Zen illustration by Pargeet S.

Zen illustration by Parjeet S.

It was NEVER about YOU…

Truth be told it never was about you. The purpose of mindfulness meditation is to find your core or center. The objective is to have easy access to that core when times are tough, and you need to lean on yourself.

Enjoy everything you do. Each mundane task when done with proper care and attention becomes a Zen meditation in itself. Breathing awareness is to create discipline from within so you can better regulate other areas of your life.

I should have addressed the book to your diaphragm as that is what it's about (pun intended).

Zen illustration by Pargeet S.

Epilogue

The current global crises we are going through is making us rethink our lives. Companies are rethinking their business models. People are considering changing their careers. A lot of irreversible damage has been done by the pandemic leading to irreparable loss. As with everything in the universe there must be and always is a bright side to the dark, the matter to the antimatter. In this situation, people were forced to break from routine and left with time they never had before to rethink what matters most.

By now you know this book is about nothing. We are trying to share whatever measly knowledge we gained from the world around us hoping it could perhaps be helpful in some small way. I would like to include few more things that are coming to my mind as I write this piece. Beauty lies in imperfection. So do not strive to be perfect or to nail mindfulness on day 1.

In Zen, the circle is never round or full. It is drawn imperfectly with a single stroke and left mostly incomplete at the top.

You need to take what you can and try to do your best to include it in your everyday life. One measly step at a time. Do not fret if you are unable to be present. Keep trying and go with the flow.

Take Away:

breathe in, breathe out…

achieving mindfulness one breath at a time

This page is unintentionally left blank because I could not delete it. Maybe I should bring my electronics back.

Made in the USA
Columbia, SC
28 April 2024